ANGEL'S DESTINY

A NOVEL STORY OF POEMS & ILLUSTRATIONS

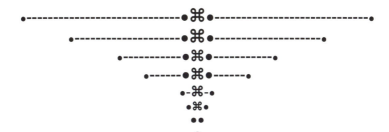

April Martin Chartrand

ANGEL'S DESTINY

A NOVEL STORY OF POEMS & ILLUSTRATIONS

Pyramid Ascension

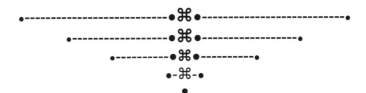

APRIL MARTIN CHARTRAND

San Francisco, California

Cover art *Pyramid Ascension*. Book design, illustrations, digital illustrations by April Martin Chartrand. Author photo by Alan Purcell.

Publisher/order: April Martin Chartrand PO Box 14752 San Francisco, CA 94114-0752 angelsdestiny2009@gmail.com http://angelsdestiny2009.blogspot.com

Permission to print the following quoted material is gratefully acknowledged: From the *Heal Your Body* by Louise Hay. Hay House Inc. ©1988. From the *You Can Heal Your Life* by Louise Hay. Hay House Inc. ©1984. From *The Meaning of Life* by Tenzin Gyatso, The XIV Dalai Lama and Jeffrey Hopkins. Wisdom Publications. ©1994 & 2000.

Library of Congress Cataloging-in-Publication Data
Chartrand, April Martin
ANGEL'S DESTINY: A Novel Story of Poems & Illustrations /
by April Martin Chartrand—1st pbk. ed./hdcov 2nd printing
p. cm.
Includes an introduction by Imani Harrington, bibliographical references, 48 illustrations, and copyright reprint permissions.

ISBN 978-061-530-2515 / ISBN 0-61-5302-51-3 (pbk./hdcov)
Poetry I. Title. 2. Illustrations–Art–Digital 3. Inspirational
4. Women's Studies–multicultural–domestic violence

Library of Congress Control Number: **2009914167**

Printed in the United States of America

FORWARD

"The divine blessing of 'Angel's Destiny' is the alchemical transformation of suffering into beautiful poetry."

—S.K. Thoth, author of *Ruby and the Tree House* (Dhejuti Records, 2009), prayformance artist, and the subject of the 2002 Academy Award winning documentary short, *Thoth.*

⌘

"This read positions you in the resting arms of an angel, and it is here, where you find redemption and destiny! Underneath a veil of poetic language is the psychological study on the reflection of truth, and what it means to live while faced with death. A slow kill that makes one think: what if our own soul was caught in a web behind the fist of destruction? In these rich and vivid poems each word hits you in the face. It is bold, lyrical and an imaginative fact and a tale that takes the reader on a spiritual journey from lies to the truth. Inside this web, is the inner nature and psyche of the once abused to a reclaimed womanist warriors' soul."

—Imani Harrington, editor of *Positive/Negative: Women of Color and HIV/AIDS* (Aunt Lute Books, 2002), writer and playwright.

⌘

"There's no excuse for domestic violence, but far too man women experience it intimately. In order to heal from this experience, women need to take steps towards inner healing and recovery."

—Esta Soler, Executive Director
Family Violence Prevention Fund, San Francisco, CA

Cosmic Symbols

April Martin Chartrand

Mirrored Ancestry

It does not matter how long we have had negative patterns, or an illness, or a rotten relationship, or lack of finances, or self-hatred, we can begin to make a change today.

Louise L. Hay, author and publisher of *Heal Your Body.*

DEDICATION
Angel Wings

To all who are embracing the difficult path of healing their life-long challenges — so that a journey of love and healing is embraced.   Choosing to change your life for the better takes dedicated inner work and courage.

April Martin Chartrand
San Francisco, CA

 CONTENTS

V: DIGITAL ILLUSTRATIONS
Illustrations digitalized in quadratic format   87-137

 ILLUSTRATIONS

INTRODUCTION

One main factor that binds one in an abusive relationship is relative to how one views herself and it is through self awareness that we are able to break through our silence. Here in 'Angel's Destiny', we find the inner working thoughts as a meditation on love and hate. A yin and yang of human behavior caught between mysticism, metaphysics and the principles of what the Gods, Goddesses, Angels and the Saints of Our Muse offers us when one uses their voice and pen as a weapon against violence. In its illustrations we find signs and symbols of transformative powers of the cosmos.

Ensconced in April Martin Chartrand's destiny we find a rare gem of a novel story of poetry that digs deep into the inner core of the soul, manifesting a deep reflection on the nature of violence. She calls on the greatest sages of our times: Thich Nhat Hanh, Dalai Lama, and even contemporaries as Louise Hay, Ruth King, Eckhart Tolle and Iyanla Vanzant all of whose philosophical underpinnings are sprinkled throughout this book and tells the tale of tension and conflict as an arc of violence and creates a spectacle with a cast of characters as told through emotions. What's key to unlocking this compendium of poetry is when the door opens on the prisoners of violence, we witness the heroic act of breaking free from ones executioner. This spiritual consciousness is verisimilitude at its best, and it offers us psychological medicine.

The poems are richly crafted in rhyme and meter and some told in the style of epigrams and others in longer stanzas that demonstrate through irony, sarcasm and wit, the illusions of anger, the attention of awareness and the offering of love where we find the archetype role each of us plays out in our own drama. Deception that hides behind violence unveils the lie of the mind and the maddening silence that traps the soul of its victims as prey. But

April Martin Chartrand

Chartrand awakens the souls of the dead and shows us how parts of ones self lost and is now found in the arms of an Angel.

Through poems like 'Angel's Destiny' we find sheer power and in *My River* Iguazú there is a self-crafted identity Goddess Siddhu that illuminates and offers inner strength and the value and strength of finding the goddess in ourselves. Chartrand tells her readers that *To Be a Poetess* is akin to being a priestess and after having been at war she comes out of battle brandishing her shield of honor and courage as redemption. This act of poetry is an allegorical spin of moral lessons for all of us.

In the last section, the most visual and reflective, she says "I've been sent here to tell you my overdue story of redemption and salvation in a world of symbolism syntax and pretext." This is a great read and metaphor reflecting historical and contemporary slavery that will reach a wide audience where we hear the cries of cultural violence and its echoes for which we have all experienced. I commend and congratulate Ms. Chartrand on her courage and character that speaks the truth about the unwavering human condition.

~Imani Harrington, Writer and Playwright
October 7, 2009

Goddess Realized

April Martin Chartrand

April Martin Chartrand

Snake Goddess

April Martin Chartrand

April Martin Chartrand

Fertility Goddess

April Martin Chartrand

xviii
April Martin Chartrand

I
ILLUSIONS

Butterfly Illusions

It is not that life is an illusion; rather, it is like an illusion. Therefore, we can speak of many different types of discrepancy between the way things appear and the way they actually exist.

Tenzin Gyatso, The XIV Dalai Lama and Jeffrey Hopkins, authors of *The Meaning of Life: The Buddhist Perspective on Cause and Effect.*

ANGEL'S DESTINY
April Martin Chartrand

WEATHERING MY ILLUSIONS

Clouds of
Mis-destined
illusions,
     dark clouds
mis-guiding
life of rainy
     illusions.

Illusions, hail-storming,
surreal-ing to thine eyes.

Struggling eyes seeking truths,
that we were put here to feel
in the depths of our
golden, rainforested souls.

Souls that yearn
indefinitely
and hope for
the sweet power
of
misty sweet love.

Love of clear days arising
and touching my beating heart,
cleansing my true spirited
     soul.

SEEING TREES

What do you see when you look at trees?
What do the rest of you see
when you look at me
as I sway in the
    breeze?

I see leaves blow in the wind's ease
that make wonderful melodic music
buzzing of bees in my ears with
    ease.

Music that swishes, crunches
and falls to the earth's ease,
rejuvenating life with bees and
colors
    freed.

What do you see?
Is it just a tree,
a sawed truth that might be
cut down replacing it with a
house perched upon a
pristine-lawned hillside
all sprayed in pea soup
green.

MY NAME IS?

Shake my hand and call me by my name.
Name has been fragmented,
name has been denied.

Don't know how to call that name yet.
Yes, my mind will answer you, but
a wounded spirit and soul emerges instead.

Desperately looking.
How do you do? Glad to meet you?
My name is _____,
and what is yours?

LIGHT OF DAY

Sullen feelings,
colliding floundering visions.

Visions once light,
now turned
to dusty gray.

Spirit illuminates dark eyes with
the light of day,
as I lay in this
misty, twisty garden
of dismay.

What Becomes Us?

No feelings left to express the
primal spirit-given endowments
abruptly
      taken away,
laying dormant inside
      breathing cadavers
until
days illuminated with pleasant revelations
melting into starry garlanded tombstones
      scattered,
            resting,
upon the earth's alchemy that provides sustenance
      for
            hungry inchworms.

WHEN

When
I
needed you,
you
were
never
      there.

When
I needed you,
little
you
begged me to
      care.

CHOOSE

Getting rid of you,
what was I supposed to do?

Getting rid of you,
something that was three years overdue.

Getting rid of you,
because you made me blacker and blue.

How do I choose?
My spirit did, to rid myself of you.

Run, hide or decide?
If you don't, you lose.
I am choosing to,
free myself of you.

ACKNOWLEDGED UNLEASHED MASKS

Acknowledge who we are,
begin to work within
    conscious circumstances.

Do not remain in your point of defeat.
Glories from above,
masks unleashed.

Renew the mind
and
actions will magnify powers of
who
we
really
are.

1492

After 1492 they came to us. The first Red American Slaves who died by diseased biological warfare.

Columbus and his vengeful 1492 sailing the oceans of red and black blood. Who Discovered you? . . .His Santa Maria?

Lincoln lasts forever . . . 1862 New Year's Emancipation Proclamation, unified hooded symbolism.
Why haven't the extermination, lynching, and cries of the first race been heard?

Announcer:
Excuse me ladies and gentlemen we have a news flash!
Excuse me ladies and gentlemen we have a news flash!
A news flash! . . . A news flash!

President Lincoln preaches to servants
Who trade in their Confederated Uniforms for
White sheets favoring their pure race . . .
Symbolizing a God of ritualized masters
Fathering the free-labored hateful
Building of the New Americas.

Announcer
This news flash has been brought to you by The Aryan Nation, the KKK, The CIA and the U.S. Government.

Thank you for listening to your own fate . . . your own fate . . . your own fate . . .

MIDDLE PASSAGE CLUES

Resisting the annoying temptation to be
    like you.
So many wasted years succumbing to the
unloving of
    you.

Splitting me in half,
becoming completely untrue.
(The they, the we, the me, and the I that really had no clue.)

To you and only
    you,
to see a slaving educated puppet that
I'd become within the likeness of
    you.

Ancient black hearts — sadly turned blue.
(What's a Goddess to do?)

Won't do this for you.
No, no, and no,
echoing oceanaut cries from
my *Middle Passage* elders with clues.

I must remove my heart and soul from you and
seek found freedoms laced with
African rhythms greater than
    you.

LOVING MY BLACKNESS

Learning and loving my Blackness
you ask,
how do you dare?

Accepting and loving my Blackness
makes you feel
why should I care?

You taught me how my mask
of an elusive Blackness
was supposed to be pretty fair.

My mysterious Blackness makes the
pale flowers ponder why
pale heads turn
and
wonder what healing beauty lies
deep inside there.

The humanness of
all
color formations of
        beauty
                thoughts.

Only
        if all felt it was
                lovely and rare.

II

ANGER

Delusions of Anger

If you let anger out and just keep expressing it, it is very difficult for this to be helpful.

Tenzin Gyatso, The XIV Dalai Lama and Jeffrey Hopkins authors of *The Meaning of Life: The Buddhist Perspective on Cause and Effect.*

FEELS LIKE HOME

Remembering the first day our breath
    met.
Remembering that hopeful day our eyes
    set.

Embraced with artistically fashioned hopes
and aspirations soon to
    forget.

Unrecognizable broken words,
words that three years later
wring the depths of my soul.

A broken heart, a broken spirit
that broken innocence
    let.

To save myself from demonic love,
soul not
    let
and must
    forget.

I remember the first day our souls met.
This feels like home,
    this feels like instinctive home.
A home full of lies, deceptions,
    and two misconceptions of
        Diabolical and hideous love.

YOU DON'T KNOW ME

You don't know me,
because I've had to live like you.
Something I no longer care to do.

You don't know me,
because I've had to be like you.

Your conditions.
        Your inhibitions.

You don't know me,
because I've had to think like you,
making my life so terribly pretend.

Your world is full of pretense,
hidden agendas, selective liberalized bigotry,
and hewed humiliations.

Your world that excludes in lieu of includes.
Refusing the very life force that summons us to create
love
unconditionally to the brim.

WHAT?

What is
it
'bout
my soul
that made you want to
take
it?

What is
it
'bout
my heart
that made you think you
could stake
it?

SICK

Never want to get sick
around you.
You never knew what to do.

When I was sick around you,
you made me feel
blacker and blue.

Screaming and yelling,
you wished
it
was not true.

Laying blame on me,
for being
       sick of you.

HAVE YOU?

Have you ever been with one
who made you sick, sick, sick? So sick,
you would pitch a fit. So pissed,
you want to hit, hit, hit. Hitting them
in places that slit, slit, slit. Slitting them
in half to see them rip, tip, rip. Ripping them
in faces that were so zip, hip, hip.

I know you're saying,
I sound like a tripping witching,
       witch,
           witch,
              which.

• ANGER •

Oh, yeah, it's been a hit, slip, trip.

ACTING

Acting with righteous indignation
at the world's
visual games of corrupt
communications.

Revealing lies that tell the truth
about your hidden
inner wounds of disdain, and
dishonor.

Every lie tells another
hidden truth.

The truth about who
you are deep inside of
the shadows of your disbelief,
suppressed,
suspended in midair, and
frozen in time.

DEMONIC LIES

Monday morning Rumor Monger's tongue lashes out
for all to see.
Painting red-tongued accusation beats of fantasy.
You did this and this . . . you did that and that . . .
a-rat-tat-tat-tat.

Rumor mongers and shit-stirrers,
        don't want peace for thee!
Yet they hide in dark places,
comforted by their muckraking glee!
People's lives are torn up by your
        vicious tornado lies,
a-rat-tat-tat-tat.

Betrayed by those who easily believe your vicious lies.
Lies that make no sense to those with civil-minded ease!
Only in the minds of the white rat
a-rat-tat-tat-tat.

These lies are all they see,
believed with hungered ease,
        simple-minded bleed.
Bleeding mouths that eat,
believe with a formal comforting disease.
A-rat-tat-tat-tat . . . rat-tat-tat-tat.

CHOKED BY THE DEMON

Breathing air
something taken for
granted.

Because you know it
will always be there.

Gasping for air,
I almost died
from panic
as demon child's
ten fingers from behind
taking my breath.

My breath
taken for
granted.

LIVING DEAD

Demons:
After the fact, seeing the signs without orgasm.
A demonic face staring directly into my eyes.
I turn away. What is wrong?
I just saw the devil and the devil is on top
and inside of me with the sword of his sexual power.
A power that makes it hard for me to see straight through
the terror I am about to embrace.
Three years in his Hell.
Who says you have to die to go to Hell
to meet the demon?
I loved, wanted, took care of him, and now have rage for
him.

Signs:
Follow our own spirit intuition.
See the patterns in behavior.
One demonic act begets another.
It is and will not be an isolated incident.
It will escalate
into something worse than you've already experienced.

One hate turns into another. Remember,
the past hate that makes a new hater hurt more than the
last?
Your subconscious will not allow you to forget what
consciousness always forgets and is not aware of anymore.
You become a life of the living dead to survive.

Unreal:
It becomes unreal.
A lie to survive.
You can't participate in life fully because you are too busy protecting, defending, and being afraid someone will find out or he will start yelling about nothing again.
The lies take over, not real, only real for fallen angels.

"Don't be negative, I am a happy person!" The *Prince of Darkness* would say after yelling about a simple issue.
"Kiss and make up." Make up what?
No resolution ever. Feelings put on hold.
Same patterns and the same behaviors.
Life of the living dead.

MY HEART

Moving too fast without love,
moving here,
moving there, and
without love,
my heart untouched,
becoming bare.

So bare,
it
cried out one night,
it cried so loud,
it jumped out and
dared.

No breath
and
dared to tell me,
     Stop it.
          Stop it.

Does anybody care?

HUMAN

We separate ourselves from others because
we are separated from ourselves,
making,
taking lives and hurting the ones who are easy targets,
a casual topic of mindless conversation,
        targeted prey.

When we hurt others we seem to forget their names.
When challenged, we are afraid to admit they possess
Mother- and father-given names.

Failing to look in the mirror of one's soul to see them,
        for who
                they
                        really
                                are.
Human days of rays.

REVELATION TRANSFORMATION

The evil of a nation can bring
burdens of sorrow upon those of us
who are naïve enough to look the other way,
hurting when the dirty deeds are upon us in a
    flash.

Revealing ourselves to the Earth Spirit
embracing a holy deity's
    sash.

Bowing at the feet of the holy,
seldom remembering earth and black ash,
hearts embracing the
sanctified spirit of "Mother Goddess's"
flowering lash.

A BRONZE AGE KAMIKAZE WORKSHOP

A *knobbed sickle,* good intensions with ill-fated missions.
Morphing cruel faces of things to come.
Crafted out of malleable elements, copper and tin.

Daggering Bronze Age kamikaze artists.
Masked workshop assistants creating folly on *Mother Goddess,*
smelting broken toys producing *Iron Maiden* hearts.

Arrowheaded dominators of their weaker subjects,
an *Age* of phallic projectiles of organized marauders,
armed with swords, dance on Heaven's teardrops.

Fashioned secular poses depicting prolific professional
warriors, holders of the Bronze Age alchemy worship,
benefactors of tarnished metallurgy
bestowed upon male spheres, and lost in wax castings.
The brand new holders of paternity vested with artillery,
marred and stolen from the ore of the *Earth Goddess.*

Spearheading, the ending of a melted magical Age.
Fertility Goddess's biological endowments
stolen from the ecstatic circled ceremonies,
altars once ornamented with clay breast spirals fall barren.

Females become the spoils of an artillery marred victor.
Hour-glass shaped biological property,
a ploughed vessel of masculine seeds,
that can no longer enter through their father's womb
orbiting the Earth's core at light speed.

SAFETY

Feelings of safety.
The mind can tell you anything it desires.
This was my time to be safe, alone, and free?
Thoughts shattered.

Calm taken away weekly by scribbled letters,
ringing of a familiar voice, accusations upon accusations.
A painted picture on unfamiliar artist's walls
and imagined mind states becoming dire.

This is my space.
The lurid lurks in the private calm of its prey.
Sacrificing mind states daily to *it* as *it* appears.
Relinquishing life and safety to those who
do not deserve *it*.
I pray.

Double Lies.
We see only what we want to believe.
        Two separate stories,
                two separate lives.
Yet, living the same hideous lie.

LIGHTING FIRES

The sacred and simple act of giving life to fire
summoned ferocious sounds in you.
A simple act, of which only you knew.

Above high, you towered with Nazi driven hate
a clenched fist,
a wrenched pointed finger.

Down below,
     I shivered,
         I quivered,
and begged for you to abate.

Your anger then, is simmered now with a
simple Goddess act of purifying
     sage.

Without you,
I've lit
my fires.
Giving me an inner power and
no longer hearing
     rage.

MANTINKO'S LINT

The Emperor of Mantinko has lint on his face,
lint on his face, lint on his face, I exclaim.

Don't you see?
All the king's jesters and all the king's men
can't put Nillie, Tillie, Manillie together again.

They all grin, as his majesty graces the little ones with
pomp and circumstance brim.
Oh, what a sin!

Court jesters all spin, grin,
and limn as the emperor glides and greets the honored
Indonesian Pacific Rim.

The court jesters prim,
the royal high court wears black shim,
never see what I see, exposed like 'lil Kim.
How grim.

I do tell,
"Excuse me, Sir; I don't think the camera will like the lint
on your lovely thick skin."
What a sin.

The Emperor of Mantinko has lint on his face,
lint on his face, I lay claim. I lay claim, I lay claim.
The press agent now royally all aflame,
the Emperor of Mantinko has lint on his face, has lint on
his face, has lint on his face, I exclaim.
                    Oh, what a grand shame!

III
AWARENESS

Goddess Awareness

You may think your mind is running the show. But that is only because you have trained your mind to think in this way.

Louise L. Hay, author and publisher of *You Can Heal Your Life*.

ANGEL'S DESTINY
April Martin Chartrand

CAN YOU HOLD A MOMENT PLEASE?

Feelings put on hold.
What mysteries will unfold?

I lay here in my place of rest,
feeling numb to what has
happened in my life.

When I speak of the evil,
I smile, as if to say, *it really did not happen to me.*
It happened to someone else.
Minimizing the pain.

Feelings.
Still not aware of the impact that
has played in my life.

Fragmentation.
When am I going to get really
angry and feel precisely what has happened
to my life?
        Simply see the reality of truth.

Fragmenting to survive.
Still here to tell the truth
of a lifetime put on hold.
Can you hold a moment please?

POPPING

Snap, Crackle, and Popping
as the delayed memories
    unfold.

Get it out,
    work it out
          or
your mind will
    explode.

MINDS OF BONITA

When one has lost one's mind,
it can be hard
to press back and
        shine.

Healing your life in time
inside a life will shine
with a heart that beats so
        fine.

But, when one is on the grind
one will see the eyes that find
the revelations in one's
        mind.

Extra Extra

"Extra, extra! Read all about it.
Spirit Woman Goddess almost dies of a broken heart."

Last month,
nearly died from
a broken heart.

All these years,
slowly dying
of a broken spirit.

Life nearly died.
(I even cried for you.)
I almost died.
      I almost died!

But
Two precious I am
plus
Two die
Four you, demon child.

TIME

Those who do not deserve the
time
caught up in their own
time.

Time
of another lonely drummer.
     A-rat-tat-tat-tat . . . tat-tat-tat.

Running and drumming to
time
that is out of time
with Goddess healing
time.
     A-rat-tat-tat-tat.

In Thoughts of You

Thoughts of you
lost myself to you.
My life squandered on a whim.
Made my life grow
       old and dim.

The thought of you
put myself out on a trembling limb.
Thoughts of you,
life was so
       grey and grim.

Un-thoughts of you
I am going to live.

TAKING IT BACK

In our silence you had power
to lie, cheat, beat, and steal.

A scene that later
became surreal.

Taking back the power of my birthright
reveals the sins of you.

Taking back my power,
I reveal to those who
        never
                knew.

WEARING HATS

Wore hats,
which engaged many places and turned many faces.
Breathed, *pill-boxed* distant
     lives.

Loved and subsisted with those who could not stop uttering
Their self-induced movie cast of tabooed
     whys.

Wore many hats, *apple caps* to *skull caps*,
and even a multi-colored dualistic *beret*.

Hats that traveled far into the
loveless wastelands of *Pandora's box*, a continual
     remiss.

To cleaning picture-perfect
stone mannequins perched on top of the Rivera's high
of an enduring self-cleaning *maid's hat* of bigoted
     hiss.

A hissing hat
hit with grit
in those lives that surely
fit in plastic places that did not feel a bit like
     it.

CONNECTING

Who are we when we connect?
This should be given
the utmost
     respect.

The stars and sky
are here to let us
     rest.

They should never
be
     suspect.

Connecting with
all eternal angelic forces, covered daily with plastic
     unrest.

That keeps us numb in techno-lives making us
     sweat.

Sweating beads of
toxic mess.

Mess that never
turns our lives into an eternal loving sweet
     success.

Resistance

Chiefs have the unyielding resistance to seeing the truth,
truth that lies dormant in shadowed black and white
subconscious remission.

Marching blindly.
Missing the embryonic days of multi-colored free truths
gone by and to come one day.

Days after living silver dimes of
carcinogenic liabilities of others.
Marching to doomed beliefs of a lipstick power minded
commander-in-chief.

Chiefs that know not of the human race.
Blindly leading her forces in drilled squared formations
down a path of black-hearted returns.

No longer marching.
Returning to witness Goddess's
lives that were being shriveled away,
squandered love, refracting talents, and untapped
prism-filled eyes now appear.

Embryonic rebirth.
Briefly glancing back at paralleled faces!
Advancing onward in an illuminating vertical
graceful stance.

FEEL

No one can tell
me
how to feel.

Even if
it is
surreal.

What's
the
deal?

Only
love
can
heal.

GRACE AT PAT'S

We are gathered together,
as the season draws near, with Pat,
her peers, and her queer musketeers.

To celebrate, give thanks
to all those so dear
we humble ourselves
to share without fear.

The life we've been given
rejoicing so clear
for gifts of daily abundance that
sustain life
and cherish so near.

We hail you infinite spirit
in the Aquarian New Year.
So cheer, my dear, and
have a great year.

PLUTO'S NEW AGE

Shooting Pluto's star,
geometric dimensionality points to the hearts and souls of
mid-Heaven's golden children,
speaking in the symbolic family language of the
fleecy *Medici's* scar.

Starburst celestial children,
purifying their past lives in burning cones of light,
orbiting Arabic parts in a neo-*Galileo's*
astrological hybrid station,
landing on purple crescent moon's star bright.

Scalding past planets of yesteryears,
incinerating themselves from the *Pope's* powerful spears,
a force permitted to fly free,
colliding with dancing deities,
          shooting stars ushering in
                    the coming of a New Age in spiral galaxies
hidden in Pluto's rising star.

A HEART IN PLACE

In time
a
beating heart
will find
its rightful place.
Don't worry it
won't take up too
        much space.

It might even beat upon your face!
Caressing time to life's ever
        changing pace.

A wise Goddess told me in
a high Indian place,
"Sista-girl, you've been looking for
your heart all these years in the
        wrong place."

Now discovering my heart in
        red earth and lace.

ANGEL'S DESTINY

We could have loved you, if you really wanted to
     know.

You could have loved the us of we and me,
if we really desired to
          grow.

As you see, I finally had to go to a healing place.
(They thought you should know.)
Two angels dressed in silvery light
flying to and fro.

Gently lifting me to Heaven's *Golden Door*,
they blessed my inner core and drank my tears away
so I shall not cry for you
          anymore.

Thus opening of colored prisms
with blessed visions of what I
          adore.

FINDING MY HEART

I traveled to a high, arid, and foreign place.
Seeking something (of which I knew of).
Something that eluded me all my life.

First time I stepped out, walking the land,
I found you lying in the dust.

You were hundreds of years old but so full of a new
acquainted wisdom, carved by the elements of time.
A perfect broken heart. A warm loving stone.

From high above, golden teardrops fell upon me.
Welcomed by the true mask of woman,
I was finally to become.
Shedding the things little girls play with.

Becoming a spirit woman has had so much pain
and
rebirthing of the heart and soul.

But now I carry the legacy of
the circled Goddess woman before me and after.

Finding my heart and soul
and
becoming a real woman for the very
first time.

68
ANGEL'S DESTINY
April Martin Chartrand

IV
LOVE

Ancient Love

Love is never outside ourselves; love is within us.

Louise L. Hay, author and publisher of *You Can Heal Your Life.*

ANGEL'S DESTINY
April Martin Chartrand

To Be a Poetess

To be a poetess,
there is a level of truth.
It comes out of me, yes (you know), like tears on a tree for
all those to be.

To be a poetess,
for I am inside of me, outside to be, I can never see
outside of me to see for thee parts of me who hide from me.

To be a poetess,
telling you a truth that one sees, taxing my
inner personal reality, slowly saving sanity from all three.
Telling cobwebbed buried multi-truths, you know
flying high with those thousand-year-old Red Trees.

To be a poetess,
will I evoke a notion of emotion in your ever reverberating
and yearning toned receptors? Will I bring the house down
in tears? My words from other worlds, that you'll try to
understand for a brief moment in time with I.

Maybe I'll never understand why, I have been sent here to
tell you my overdue story of redemption and salvation in a
world of symbolism, syntax, and pretext.

To be a poetess,
I want to be free to sing with glee. My words of under!

Only if all could see and wonder, reaching out to you and into me. The many me's inside so free.

• LOVE •

THINKING

I don't feel
lost
when I think about
         You.

I
feel
keen and clear.

What about
         You?

HEART OF THANKS

In my heart of beating hearts.
An abundance of gratitude to you for
unearthing purple flowers
of an ancient circled *womanness*.

A *womanness* that is reminiscent
of a revealing political stance by
Judy Chicago.
Can you guess, *Who Is Coming to Dinner?*

Your pure loving deeds, and
carefully transcribed scriptures of a
wise and noble heart.

Chiseling away patiently
at my multi-faceted stone exterior.
Now taking on true artistic form.

A smiling light shines inside my heart.
Light that shines brightly through
a newly, painstakingly guided self.

YOUR MAGICAL KISS

African Renaissance and Celtic lace,
glide into an enchanted temple of creation.
A ritual begins.

Your magical kiss.
Receptive, unconscious lips weaving radiant reawakenings,
solving mysterious questions of what it means to be alive.

Your magical kiss.
Enraptured interplay of adoration and desire
beckoning forth my once squandered woman-spirit
now ascending lavish beauty,
loose and light, beaming enchanted heavenly delights.

Your magical kiss.
Flying amidst herbal potions guided by
silver *cords*, nourishing honeyed lips.
Tempered juices animating divine vessels
dancing to living beats.

Your magical kiss.
Spellbound by sweet electrical tarried time,
pulsing to dynamic interplays
of ecstatic reverent mist.

Our magical kiss.
A ritual ends.
One that shall be missed.

WRESTLING WITH SCOTT

Wrestling hearts, symphonic poems matched,
being, breathing, and beating
tunes in treble clefs melodically
crooning black and white time.

Time metered, a soul with kind and generous visions
listening to duets
gracing finger tips on fine-tuned bodied visions.

Melodies of breathing music in my ears,
a heartbeat that saved my fears.
Not remembering why, reaching out, and
becoming vulnerable to a face that appears to be
bigger than *I*.

I who now play scales (couplets of sorts)
with Mozart's prodigy and his musical consorts.
Shining light, melodically whispering in my
triple-timed heart and dreams.

Light pianissimo sonatas breathing in the eyes of his
mentors,
glowing fingers serenading every pore of my body.
Surrendering to every beat of his touch.

I melt in tempo,
a rest, a refrain, a signature,
cooled by sea-breezed Gregorian enchanted nights,
sprinkling its essence on new orchestrated rebirths.

In Memory of L. G.

Our passionate life of art and dance brought us together,
as brother and sister
of a spiritual kind.

By a simple act of alchemical ink and tree bark.
Listening to our soon to meet inner-voices
of dancing visions and ballet's color hues in
theatrical viewing room for all to see.

Your gifted vision to
live a life of the quintessential renaissance man
gave me strength in my desperate days to hold on to
my nearly fading life.

You had so little to hold on to
but fought desperately to be part of a life that
could not understand the why of it all.
For they don't understand thus they don't know.

But I know you are choreographing the heavens
in *Full Extension* and on *Beauty's Point,* talking at
Heaven's door with Alvin Ailey and all the rest.

You are in the company of exceptional greats.
Your long days and nights of quiet unrest
are now blessed with the joy of Heaven's love of Angels
and graceful Goddesses who will give you the peace you
adore.
Until we meet again at *Heaven's Door* . . .
     Your loving sister.

KEALAKEKUA BAY DOLPHINS OF KONA

Dolphins in the silvery blue liquid light,
may your days be
bright.

Illuminating radiant sights
spinning and flying to new
heights.

Dynamic duos of terrestrial chatter-boxes
somersaulting in the anointed sea-breezed air
of *Pali Kapu O Keōua*'s blessed
site.

Kealakekua: "The God's Pathway."
Pali Kapu O Keōua: The burial place of Hawaiian royalty
on a steep cliff that is on the coast of Kona, HI.

THE LIFE BOAT

Once perched
 on a mountain top,
 an anointed navigational vessel
 in the *Land of Gospels.*

Now lost at sea.
 Survivors
 seeking the safety and splendor
 of the One who mothers/fathers miracles,
 calms the storms,
 feeds hungry thousands
 by the *Sea of Galilee.*

FOR YOU . . . A SPECIAL PLACE IN MY HEART

Overshadowed
in a desperate struggle
to
save urgent life.

You awarded something
that was struggling to be
and
without *it*, it could never be.

You presented me with
a great love
that had eluded me,
a new woman
who had hidden from view,
and a determination,
that had almost faded.

I will be forever yours
and
have provided a special place
in my willing heart
for the beauty in you.

REFLECTIONS

Do I mirror You?
An element, only a few can do.

Sheltered secrets,
if only
the rest really knew.

Opening of the
            heart and soul
makes one
run and skip like
            new.

New crystal mirrored
reflections
of a peaceful chosen
            few.

A few who appear
as the me
in
the mirror of
            You.

SETTING STANDARDS

Who are you?
Are you the you that is in the
I?

The I who
knows standards of
artistic beauty.

A beautiful angelic
radiance of inner love
that sets the stage for
happy endings and
birthing
new beginnings.

Dreaming of
two golden angels lifting me
high above the
watery mountain top
of a
candlelit *Mont Saint Michel.*

Le Mont Saint Michele: A Monastery on an isolated tidal
island on the Normandy coast of France.

MY RIVER OF IGUAZÚ

My vision holds close to your phallic embrace.
As Heaven inscribes lunar messages across
oceanic sunset skies.

I am *Siddhu*, birthed from the fertile riverbanks of the
Iguazú.
Possessing ancient mysterious gifts of alchemical
invocations emanating from the sacred Neolithic religions,
evoking ancient mysteries, and rising out of Paleolithic
beginnings.
Religions are sustained in paradigmatic serpentine
megaliths that kiss the sky.

I am enlightened without physical presence.
A magnificence of deep traditions possessing voluptuous
majestic abilities, communicated through holy medicinal
ground, and streaming sacred juices into the mouth of our
creation.

You yearn for my impassioned embrace
and to drink the honey of eternal, pink, glistening gifts,
unconsciously propelled to partake in my cascading juices,
and held gently in forested and drenched pink lips.

But, indebted to your male-adapted apparitions, illusions,
delusions of a new-century conquistador,
and masqueraded in cephalic subjugation,
this rips your heart and closes your spirit to this
ethnodynastic-Goddess before you.

A vessel of pulsating waters contained within
bodied visions of mystic re-birth.

Swirling, whirling, and spiraling, serpentined arteries create
the river of the Iguazú, laced in black folds of glistening
pink invite.
A chain of vibrations sustained in female vulva,
realms of eternal midnight hued fern orchards,
spiraling and snaking through the generous jungles of
copper-colored rich essential ancestral minerals,
92 simple building blocks of cosmic universal creation,
embraced in jeweled waters from the melodic lips of
restoration, and leading you to the mouth of sweet
anticipation.

Parting lips beckon the expanding universe of my
Queen's Chamber. Melting into my stream of life,
mystical giver of all things blessed.
Transformed by dramatic reflections sharing experiences of
    cosmic revelations.

Revealing rhythms that unite our heartbeats in my
passioned *Queen's Chamber*:
By sitting, breathing in Tantric poses of mystic fire,
commissioned by the divine love of Isis
and the protection of *Quan Yin*, breathing in powerful
metaphors nourishing thirsty hearts,
creating an unexpected mystic fire,
melting into deep realms of primal bliss evoking states of
relaxation, revelation, and resuscitation.

I am *Siddhu,* birthed from the fertile riverbanks of the
Iguazú.
Possessing ancient mysterious gifts of alchemical
invocations emanating from sacred Neolithic religions
evoking
ancient mysteries.

I am no longer a mere sexual fugitive from my form,
nor fearful as to the nature of my creation.
For I am a chain of vibrations returning you home,
returning you home,
      from your *Homeric Odyssey.*
Unearthed in the female realms of the eternal rivers of
Iguazú.
Fusing human form with the cosmic *Almighty-All*
and
      blessed by the maker of our Creation.

Iguazú also spelled *Iguaçu*: The South American Iguazu
River is located on the border of the Brazilian state of
Paraná and the Argentine province of Misiones.
Siddhu: A river Goddess, my invention.
Quan Yin: Goddess of compassion and mercy.
Queen's Chamber: A chamber within the Pyramid of Giza,
Egypt.

ANGEL'S DESTINY
April Martin Chartrand

GODDESS MODELING

A day will come when you'll never say,
"I know you but I forgot to gaze into your eyes".
Eyes that tell tales of a wo-man's scorn, an invisible, black
African wo-man.

Holding onto a life that forces
painting her hands full of unrelenting
sorrows, disappointments, and many regrets of
the superior Western civilized institutions which look
outside of her eyes to tell her how *models*
should truly
    feel.

Forgetting to gaze into the eyes of the soul to see if she is
    alive.
Who will see if she is really alive and fully feel a human
spirit?
    Red-blooded, same as you and me.

All dressed up like exceptionally
great tasting wine and culinary delights.
Eloquently modeling voodoo dances of her elders
through a sacred space in
    time.

A time that will never dine on
      black-bottoms and wine.

GODDESS LA CASA

Beautiful Goddess wo-man.
So many
    unlived lives.

Stonehenge lives illuminated by lunar constellations,
observed from solar temples on high.
Never forgetting the magnetic energy in
    God's eyes.

Slumbering eyes outside refusing to see
mythologically-mirrored life and birth,
mirrored reflections in a moon Goddess'
    untold cries.

Majestic serpent priestesses,
embodying voluptuous divine vessels,
bringing forth preordained creations
before the altar of the
    Great Mother's eyes.

Creative innerforces
    of
Goddess's chandeliered beauty
    rebirthing glistening lives.

UNKNOWING SPIRIT GODDESS

The unknowing spirit Goddess, in that she knew.
That moved her flesh in silent prayers of
melodic hypnotic grooves.

Once, a freaky Goddess that made them stare
drew them to her hidden beauty and proclaimed
"Your majesty, you are aware."

Unknowingly, actualizing whispered dreams
of silent voices, intuition, premonitions
and
the eeriness of *déjà vu.*

Now choosing,
listening to inner voices,
and moving through
inner choices.

V
DIGITAL ILLUSTRATIONS

Butterfly Pyramid #2

ANGEL'S DESTINY
April Martin Chartrand

88
ANGEL'S DESTINY
April Martin Chartrand

Butterfly Pyramid #3

89
ANGEL'S DESTINY
April Martin Chartrand

◆DIGITAL ILLUSTRATIONS◆

90
ANGEL'S DESTINY
April Martin Chartrand

Butterfly Pyramid #4

91
ANGEL'S DESTINY
April Martin Chartrand

92
ANGEL'S DESTINY
April Martin Chartrand

Pyramid Ascension #3

93
ANGEL'S DESTINY
April Martin Chartrand

94
ANGEL'S DESTINY
April Martin Chartrand

Pyramid Ascension #4

95
ANGEL'S DESTINY
April Martin Chartrand

96
ANGEL'S DESTINY
April Martin Chartrand

Pyramid Ascension #5

97
ANGEL'S DESTINY
April Martin Chartrand

98
ANGEL'S DESTINY
April Martin Chartrand

•DIGITAL ILLUSTRATIONS•

Pyramid Ascension #6

99
ANGEL'S DESTINY
April Martin Chartrand

◆DIGITAL ILLUSTRATIONS◆

100
ANGEL'S DESTINY
April Martin Chartrand

Cosmic Symbols #2

101
ANGEL'S DESTINY
April Martin Chartrand

Mirrored Ancestry #2

103
ANGEL'S DESTINY
April Martin Chartrand

104
ANGEL'S DESTINY
April Martin Chartrand

Angel Wings #2

105
ANGEL'S DESTINY
April Martin Chartrand

106
ANGEL'S DESTINY
April Martin Chartrand

Eye See Wadjet #2

107
ANGEL'S DESTINY
April Martin Chartrand

◆DIGITAL ILLUSTRATIONS◆

108
ANGEL'S DESTINY
April Martin Chartrand

Pyramid Prayers #2

109
ANGEL'S DESTINY
April Martin Chartrand

ANGEL'S DESTINY
April Martin Chartrand

Goddess Realized #2

ANGEL'S DESTINY
April Martin Chartrand

Goddess Realized #3

113
ANGEL'S DESTINY
April Martin Chartrand

114
ANGEL'S DESTINY
April Martin Chartrand

Spiral Snake Goddess #2

115
ANGEL'S DESTINY
April Martin Chartrand

116
ANGEL'S DESTINY
April Martin Chartrand

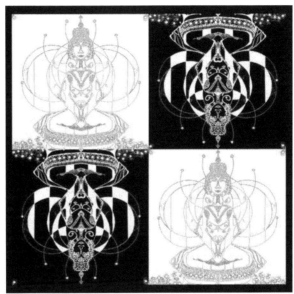

Fertility Goddess #2

118
ANGEL'S DESTINY
April Martin Chartrand

Fertility Goddess #3

ANGEL'S DESTINY
April Martin Chartrand

120
ANGEL'S DESTINY
April Martin Chartrand

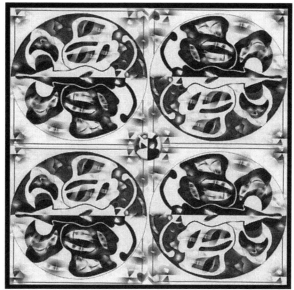

Butterfly Illusions #2

121
ANGEL'S DESTINY
April Martin Chartrand

122
ANGEL'S DESTINY
April Martin Chartrand

Delusions of Anger #2

124
ANGEL'S DESTINY
April Martin Chartrand

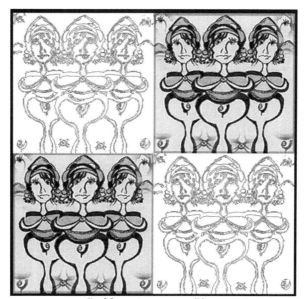

Goddess Awareness #2

ANGEL'S DESTINY
April Martin Chartrand

126
ANGEL'S DESTINY
April Martin Chartrand

Ancient Love #2

127
ANGEL'S DESTINY
April Martin Chartrand

128
ANGEL'S DESTINY
April Martin Chartrand

Me, Myself, and I #2

129
ANGEL'S DESTINY
April Martin Chartrand

130
ANGEL'S DESTINY
April Martin Chartrand

Southern Women of the Nûñnë'hï

ANGEL'S DESTINY
April Martin Chartrand

The Mother & Father in My Dreams #2

133
ANGEL'S DESTINY
April Martin Chartrand

134
ANGEL'S DESTINY
April Martin Chartrand

The Mother & Father in My Dreams #3

ANGEL'S DESTINY
April Martin Chartrand

136
ANGEL'S DESTINY
April Martin Chartrand

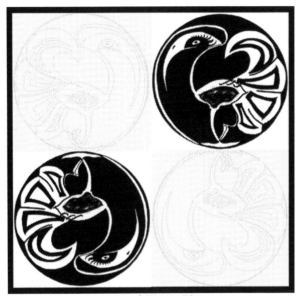

Angel Wings #2

137
ANGEL'S DESTINY
April Martin Chartrand

ANGEL'S DESTINY
April Martin Chartrand

PERMISSIONS

Grateful acknowledgment is made to the following publishers:

vii:
Hay, Louise L., Author/Publisher. *Heal Your Body: The Mental Causes for Physical Illness and the Metaphysical Way to Overcome Them,* ©1988. Hay House Inc. Carlsbad, CA 92018: p. 3.

I – ILLUSIONS:
Gyatso, Tenzin, The XIV Dalai Lama and Hopkins, Jeffrey, ©1994 & 2000. Reprinted from *The Meaning of Life: The Buddhist Perspective on Cause and Effect.* Wisdom Publications 199 Elm Street, Somerville, MA 02144 USA. www.wisdompubs.org: p. 29.

II – ANGER:
Gyatso, Tenzin, Ibid: p. 50.

III – AWARENESS:
Hay, Louise L. *You Can Heal Your Life,* ©1984. Hay House Inc., Carlsbad, CA 92018: p. 71.

IV – LOVE:
Hay, Louise L., Ibid: p. 105.

A TREASURE CHEST OF BOOKS & TAPES

Here is a list of few phenomenal and relevant books for further illumination.

I – ILLUSIONS

Bradshaw, John. *Bradshaw on: The Family: A Revolutionary Way to Self-Discovery.* (Health Communications, Inc.).

Ruiz, Don Miguel. *The Four Agreements: A Practical Guide to Personal Freedom.* (Amber-Allen Publishing, Inc., 1997).

Tolle, Eckhart. *A New Earth: Awakening to Your Life's Purpose.* (Plume-Penguin Group, 2006).

Vanzant, Iyanla. *In the Meantime: Finding Yourself and the Love You Want.* (Simon & Schuster Adult Publishing Group, 1998).

II – ANGER

Hanh, Thich Nhat. *Anger: Wisdom for Cooling the Flames.* (Riverhead, 2002).

Hay, Louise L. *You Can Heal Your Life.* (Hay House, Inc., 2005).

King, Ruth. *Healing Rage - Women Making Inner Peace Possible.* (Gotham, 2007).

Myss, Caroline. *Why People Don't Heal and How They Can.* (Sound True, 2001).

III – AWARENESS

Kornfield, Jack. *A Path with Heart.* (Bantam, 1993).

Vanzant, Iyanla. *Acts of Faith.* (Fireside/Simon & Schuster, 1993).

Zinn, Howard. *A People's History of the United States 1492–Present.* (Harper-Collins Publishers, 1999).

Zukav, Gary. *The Seat of the Soul.* (Fireside, 1989).

IV – LOVE

Carlson, Richard and Shield, Benjamin. *Handbook for the Soul & Handbook for the Heart.* (One Spirit, 1997).

Hanh, Thich Nhat. *The Heart of the Buddha's Teaching.* (Parallax Press, 1998).

Ruiz, Don Miguel. *The Mastery of Love: A Practical Guide to the Art of Relationships.* (Amber-Allen Publishing, 1999).

Sjoo, Monica and Mor, Barbara. *The Great Cosmic Mother.* (Harper & Row, 1987).

PREVIOUSLY PUBLISHED

All of the poems in this book have been revised and edited in 2009. Previous title versions by April Martin Chartrand appear in the following:

"Heart of Thanks." San Diego, CA: *Promo Trends/African American Women on Tour Newsletter,* April 1998: p. 3.

"Taking it Back." San Francisco, CA: *New Mission News,* June 1997: p. 21.

"Reflections." Nashville, TN: *Anthology of Christian Poetry.* Ed. Kathryn E. Darden, 1997: p. 80.

"Your Magical Kiss." Carmel, CA: *Creative With Words Publications.* Ed. Britta Gelrich, Vol. *The Stuff Traditions Are Made of,* 1997: p. 53.

"Angel's Destiny." Carmel, CA: *Creative With Words Publications.* Ed. Britta Gelrich, Vol. *Fly Away!* 1997: p. 59.

"Thinking of You." Carmel, CA: *Creative With Words Publications.* Ed. Britta Gelrich, Vol. *Love,* 1996: p. 7.

"Feel." San Francisco, CA: *City of Refuge Community Church Announcements & Calendar.* May 26, 1996: p. 2.

"In Memory of L. G." Oakland, CA: *Whazzup! Magazine,* Vol. 1, Issue 5, September 1996: p. 5.

"Goddess Modeling." San Francisco, CA: *Dykespeak*, June 1995: p. 46.

"Sick." San Francisco, CA: *Women Against Imperialism* (WAI News), Fall/Winter 1994, Issue 2: p. 6.

"Lighting Fires." San Francisco, CA: *Women Against Imperialism* (WAI News): Fall/Winter 1994, Issue 2: p. 6.

ANGEL'S DESTINY
April Martin Chartrand

AUTHOR'S BIBLIOGRAPHY

Bay Area Business Woman. "San Francisco Mental Health Board Appoints New Member — April Martin Chartrand." Berkeley, CA: *Bay Area Business Woman*, April 1997: p. 20.

Chartrand, April Martin, Visual Artist. "Buddha's Corners" (Digital Collage). Berkeley, CA: *Turning Wheel: The Journal of Socially Engaged Buddhism*, Summer 2003: p. 3.

Chartrand, April Martin. "Beyond Culture and Cultural Competency." San Francisco, CA: *Bay Area Reporter* (Guest Opinion), Vol. 27, Num. 18, May 1, 1997: p. 8.

Chartrand, April Martin. "Remembering the Violence." Oakland, CA: *The Oakland Tribune*, August 11, 1993: p. A-10.

Grambs, Marya, Author, Ed. Martin, Sue. "Think How Your Life Would Have Been Different If Someone Had Helped You." San Francisco, CA: *Family Violence Prevention Fund*, 1997: p. 2.

Hetzner, Amy. "S.F. Rally Focuses On Abuse Survivors." San Francisco, CA: *San Francisco Examiner*, June 28, 1994: p. A-10.

Hulsen, Amy. "The Art of Healing-Woman uses Creativity to Mend the Scars of Violence — April Martin Chartrand, Artist/Survivor." San Francisco, CA: *San Francisco State University Golden Gater*, October 28, 1997: p. 1.

Joiner, Lottie. "The Right Chemistry — April Martin Chartrand, Artist." Washington, DC: *Emerge Magazine*, November 1999: p. 14.

Reisberg, Beth Dora. "Women on the Path." Berkeley, CA: *Psychic Reader*, Vol. 22, Num. 6, June 1997: p. 7-8.

San Francisco Frontiers News Magazine. "Whole Life Expo April 25-27 — April Martin Chartrand." San Francisco, CA: *San Francisco Frontiers News Magazine* (Baylife Section), Vol. 15, Num. 26, April 24, 1997: p. 38.

ANGEL'S DESTINY
April Martin Chartrand

Me, Myself, and I

ANGEL'S DESTINY
April Martin Chartrand

ACKNOWLEDGEMENTS

Southern Women of the Nûññë'hï

To my wonderful art teacher Verity Dierauf at City College of San Francisco. Her class offered me an opportunity to draw all of the images that appear in this book. What a wonderful semester of exploration in art and spiritual journeys.

My deepest gratitude to a kind hearted S.K. Thoth for professional editorial assistance and writer/playwright Ms. Imani Harrington for her instructive peer review, women's sensibilities, and valuable editing suggestions which helped me fine-tune these poems. To the "William Shakespeare of Soap Opera Writers", Mr. Patrick Mulcahey for his generous gift and extraordinary editing. Thank you to all who have offered a kind word or deed which supported me along a challenging life path. Finally, to a dedicated Cowboy for his belonging and support.

ANGEL'S DESTINY
April Martin Chartrand

NOTES

The Mother & Father in my Dreams

This book was created partly in Adobe Photoshop 7.0 and Microsoft Word, is set in Times New Roman and Felix Tilting. All of the initial illustration renderings were by hand then redesigned in Adobe Photoshop 7.0.

AUTHOR'S BIOGRAPHY

April Martin Chartrand's articles and poems have been published in the *Bay Area Reporter, Oakland Tribune, Whazzup! Magazine*, and *Family Violence Prevention Fund's:* "Think How Your Life Would Have Been Different If Someone Had Helped You."

She has been featured on KQED Radio's *Forum*, KPOO Radio, KTVU TV 10:00 p.m. News, KRON *Bay Area Back Roads* and KTVU TV *Bay Area People*.

Chartrand is a national award-winning fiberalchemist. Her art work is displayed in the Atlanta Life Insurance Company's private collection. July 1, 1997 was *April Martin Chartrand Day* an honorary Proclamation issued by former San Francisco Mayor Willie Lewis Brown Jr.

The City and County Commission on the Status of Women awarded Chartrand with the 1998 *Isabelle Cerna Award*, San Francisco Board of Supervisors *Certificate of Honor* (1998/2001), and a San Francisco Public Library *Unsung Hero Award* presented by Supervisor Sophie Maxwell in 2001.

Chartrand holds a B.A. in Creative Arts (Center for the Experimental Interdisciplinary Arts) from San Francisco State University.

angelsdestiny2009@gmail.com
http://angelsdestiny2009.blogspot.com/
http://www.youtube.com/user/AprilMartinChartrand

Author photograph by Alan Purcell

Pyramid Ascension #2

ANGEL'S DESTINY
April Martin Chartrand

Angel Wings #2

151
ANGEL'S DESTINY
April Martin Chartrand

Order Signed Copies:
April Martin Chartrand
PO Box 14752 San Francisco, CA 94114-0752
Email: angelsdestiny2009@gmail.com

$13.00 plus $3.99 (USA) shipping and handling/tax-
Send: Money order only (no checks accepted)
Include your email and personalization name (print)

Visit me on the web:
http://angelsdestiny2009.blogspot.com/
http://www.youtube.com/user/AprilMartinChartrand
http://www.redroom.com/member/aprilmartinchartrand
http://www.myspace.com/aprilmartinchartrand
Facebook Fan: April Martin Chartrand

Made in the United States of America

$13.00
ISBN-10:   0-615-30251-3
ISBN-13: 978-0-615-30251-5
51300>

9 780615 302515